Healthy Kitchen™

Eggs

Contents

When you see these symbols:

 Tells you the SmartPoints value per serving

 Indicates a recipe is gluten free

 Indicates a recipe is vegetarian

 Indicates a recipe is nut free

 Indicates a recipe is dairy free

THE SMALL PRINT

EGGS We use medium eggs, unless otherwise stated. Pregnant women, the elderly and children should avoid recipes with eggs which are raw or not fully cooked if not produced under the British Lion code of practice.

FRUIT AND VEGETABLES Recipes use medium-size fruit and veg, unless otherwise stated.

REDUCED-FAT SOFT CHEESE Where a recipe uses reduced-fat soft cheese, we mean a soft cheese with 30% less fat than its full-fat equivalent.

LOW-FAT SPREAD When a recipe uses a low-fat spread, we mean a spread with a fat content of no more than 39%.

MICROWAVES If we have used a microwave in any of our recipes, the timings will be for an 850-watt microwave oven.

PREP AND COOK TIMES These are approximate and meant to be guidelines only. Prep time includes all steps up to and following the main cooking time(s). Stated cook times may vary according to your oven.

VEGETARIAN Recipes displaying a vegetarian symbol include non-meat ingredients, but may also contain processed products that aren't always vegetarian, such as pesto. If you're a vegetarian, you should ensure you use vegetarian varieties and check the ingredients labels. Where we reference vegetarian Italian-style hard cheese in vegetarian recipes, we mean a cheese similar to Parmesan (which is not vegetarian) but which is suitable for vegetarians.

VEGAN Recipes displaying a vegan symbol include no products made from or with the aid of animals or animal products.

GLUTEN FREE Recipes labelled as gluten free include ingredients that naturally do not contain gluten, but may also contain processed products, such as sauces, stock cubes and spice mixes. If so, you should ensure that those products do not include any gluten-containing ingredients (wheat, barley or rye) – these will be highlighted in the ingredients list on the product label. Manufacturers may also indicate whether there is a chance their product may have been accidentally contaminated with gluten during the manufacturing process. For more information and guidance on gluten-free products, visit www.coeliac.org.uk

NUT FREE Recipes displaying a nut free symbol include ingredients that do not contain nuts, but may include ingredients produced in facilities that also handle nut products. If you have a nut allergy, check ingredients labels for more information.

DAIRY FREE Recipes displaying a dairy free symbol include ingredients that naturally do not contain dairy, but may include ingredients produced in facilities that also handle dairy products. If you have a dairy allergy, check ingredients labels for more information.

SMARTPOINTS® have been calculated using the values for generic foods, not brands (except where stated). Tracking using branded items may affect the recorded SmartPoints.

Packed with protein, simple to cook and incredibly versatile, eggs are a must-have ingredient – if you have a few eggs to hand, you'll never be short of a tasty meal. Whether they're simply poached on toast, soft-boiled in a classic Niçoise salad or part of a sauce in a spaghetti carbonara, eggs take the starring role in the delicious dishes in this cookbook. Inside you'll find 36 cracking recipes that make the most of this amazing food – some are tried and tested favourites; others might take you by surprise. Best of all, eggs are a ZeroPoint™ food, so you can enjoy them for breakfast, lunch or dinner, knowing you're making the most of your SmartPoints Budget.

Turkey, egg & avo breakfast

serves 2   **prep time** 5 minutes   **cook time** 6 minutes

2 x 40g slices granary bread

¼ avocado, peeled and stone removed

2 slices wafer thin turkey

1 tomato, thickly sliced

2 eggs

Rocket leaves, to serve

1   Toast the bread.

2   In a small bowl, mash the avocado, then spread it over the toast. Top with a slice of wafer-thin turkey and a slice of tomato.

3   Crack the eggs into a pan of simmering water and poach for about 3 minutes until the whites are just set and the yolks are still soft. Remove from the pan with a slotted spoon and drain on a plate lined with kitchen paper.

4   Put a poached egg on top of each toast slice. Season to taste and serve with some rocket on the side.

Cook's tip
Add another poached egg for no extra SmartPoints.

 5   SmartPoints value per serving

Mushroom Florentine omelette

serves 1 prep time 15 minutes cook time 15 minutes

Calorie controlled cooking spray

½ small onion, finely sliced

1 garlic clove, crushed

75g button mushrooms, quartered

75g chestnut mushrooms, quartered

1 portobello mushroom, thickly sliced

50g young leaf spinach

2 eggs

50ml skimmed milk

1 tablespoon chopped fresh flat-leaf parsley, plus extra leaves, to serve

20g ricotta

1 teaspoon grated vegetarian Italian-style hard cheese, to serve

1 Mist a large nonstick frying pan with cooking spray and set over a medium-high heat. Add the onion and cook, stirring, for 6-8 minutes or until softened. Add the garlic and all of the mushrooms and cook, stirring, for 5 minutes until the mushrooms are golden. Add the spinach and cook for 1 minute until wilted. Remove the pan from the heat, season to taste and set aside.

2 Whisk together the eggs, milk and chopped parsley in a large jug until combined, then season to taste. Lightly mist a small nonstick frying pan with cooking spray and set over a medium-high heat. Pour the egg mixture into the pan and cook for 30 seconds or until the base is set. Using a spatula, draw the edges of the omelette into the centre to allow the uncooked egg mixture to run underneath. Cook for a further 2-3 minutes or until almost set.

3 Spoon the mushroom mixture over half the omelette, then dot over the ricotta. Fold the omelette over to enclose the filling.

4 Slide the omelette onto a plate and serve topped with the extra parsley leaves and the grated cheese.

Cook's tip
A flexible silicone spatula is ideal for making omelettes and helping to move the mixture around the pan.

3 SmartPoints value per serving

Black bean shakshuka

serves 4   **prep time 15 minutes**   **cook time 30 minutes**

Calorie controlled cooking spray

1 onion, finely diced

½ teaspoon each fennel and cumin seeds

2 garlic cloves, crushed

1 red chilli, deseeded and finely diced

1 teaspoon smoked paprika

¼ teaspoon cayenne pepper

1 red and 1 yellow pepper, each deseeded and finely sliced

Grated zest of ½ lemon

2 x 400g tins chopped tomatoes

400g tin black beans, drained and rinsed

75g young leaf spinach

4 eggs

30g light feta, crumbled, to serve

3 tablespoons chopped fresh flat-leaf parsley, to serve

1. Mist a large nonstick frying pan with cooking spray. Set over a medium heat, then add the onion, fennel and cumin seeds and cook for 6-8 minutes until the onion is soft. Add a splash of water if it starts to stick.

2. Add the garlic and chilli and cook for another 2-3 minutes. Add the ground spices and peppers, frying until the peppers are just soft. Stir in the grated lemon zest and tomatoes, then simmer for 5 minutes.

3. Add the beans and spinach and season to taste. Bring to the boil for 5 minutes, then reduce the heat. Create four wells in the sauce and crack an egg into each. Cook for 5 minutes, uncovered, then for 2 minutes, covered, until the whites of the eggs are set but the yolks are still runny.

4. Serve topped with the crumbled feta and chopped parsley.

 SmartPoints value per serving

Cook's tip
Serve this with 50g French bread per person for an extra 3 SmartPoints per serving.

Bacon, egg & sausage burger

serves 2   **prep time 10 minutes**   **cook time 15 minutes**

Calorie controlled cooking spray
2 x 125g reduced-fat sausages
4 bacon medallions
2 plum tomatoes, halved lengthways
2 eggs
2 x 60g slices ciabatta, split
20g young leaf spinach
2 tablespoons tomato chutney

1 Mist a large nonstick frying pan with cooking spray and set over a medium-high heat. Add the sausages and bacon, and cook, turning occasionally, for 8-10 minutes or until the sausages are cooked though and the bacon is crisp. Slice the sausages thinly. Transfer to a plate with the bacon and cover to keep warm. Put the tomatoes in the pan and cook for 1-2 minutes on each side or until tender. Transfer to a plate and set aside.

2 Wipe the pan clean, mist with more cooking spray and set over a medium heat. Crack in the eggs and fry for 3 minutes or until cooked to your liking.

3 Toast the bread. Top each base with spinach, tomatoes, sausage, bacon, egg and chutney. Sandwich with the bread tops and serve.

9 SmartPoints value per serving

Veggie hash with poached eggs

serves 4 **prep time** 15 minutes **cook time** 40 minutes

600g new potatoes, larger ones halved

2 courgettes, trimmed, halved lengthways and sliced on the diagonal

1 yellow pepper, deseeded and sliced into thin wedges

Calorie controlled cooking spray

1 teaspoon chopped fresh thyme leaves, plus extra leaves to garnish

1 red onion, sliced into thin wedges

200g cherry tomatoes, halved

4 large eggs

Small handful fresh basil, finely chopped, plus extra leaves to garnish

Small handful fresh flat-leaf parsley, finely chopped

Freshly ground black pepper

1 Cook the potatoes in a pan of boiling water for 10 minutes until just tender. Drain and leave to dry.

2 In a large bowl, combine the courgettes and pepper, mist with cooking spray and toss together with the thyme.

3 Mist a large nonstick pan with cooking spray, then cook the onion until soft, about 6-8 minutes, over a medium-low heat. Add the potatoes, courgettes and pepper and season to taste. Add a splash of water, lower the heat, and cover; cook for 15 minutes, until the potatoes are cooked through.

4 Remove the lid, increase the heat to high and cook, stirring, for 4 minutes until the veg starts to char. Transfer to a bowl and put the tomatoes in the pan. Cook, stirring, for 1 minute until softened. Return all the veg to the pan and set aside.

5 Meanwhile, crack the eggs into a pan of simmering water and poach for about 3 minutes until the whites are just set and the yolks are still soft. Remove from the pan with a slotted spoon and drain on a plate lined with kitchen paper. Toss the herbs through the veg, then serve topped with the eggs, the extra thyme and basil and freshly ground black pepper.

Cook's tip

Like it spicy? Add a dash of Tabasco sauce when serving, for no extra SmartPoints.

 SmartPoints value per serving

Breakfast frittata

serves 2 **prep time** 10 minutes + resting **cook time** 30 minutes

100g baby new potatoes, sliced

3 eggs

1 tablespoon chopped fresh flat-leaf parsley

Calorie controlled cooking spray

1 red onion, cut into wedges

4 bacon medallions, chopped

50g mushrooms, sliced

5 cherry tomatoes, halved

1 Put the potatoes in pan of cold water and bring to the boil. Cook for 10 minutes until tender. Drain and set aside.

2 Meanwhile, whisk the eggs together with 1 teaspoon cold water and the parsley. Season to taste.

3 Put a small nonstick frying pan over a medium heat and mist with cooking spray. Add the onion and cook for 5 minutes until golden, then transfer to the bowl with the eggs. Fry the bacon in the pan for 1-2 minutes, then add to the egg mixture.

4 Mist the pan with more cooking spray and fry the mushrooms for 2-3 minutes until tender. Add them to the egg mixture, along with the potato, and stir to combine.

5 Mist the pan with more cooking spray, then put the egg and veg mixture in the pan and cook over a medium heat for 4 minutes. Meanwhile, heat the grill to high. Top the frittata with the halved cherry tomatoes and grill for 4-5 minutes, until the egg is set and golden.

6 Leave the frittata to rest for 5 minutes (this makes it easier to slice), then slide it onto a board and cut into 4 wedges. Serve 2 wedges per person.

Cook's tip

You can use whatever zero SmartPoints vegetables and herbs you like – or whatever you have in the fridge!

2 SmartPoints value per serving

Scrambled eggs & spinach on rye

serves 2   **prep time** 5 minutes   **cook time** 5 minutes

Calorie controlled cooking spray
6 spring onions, trimmed and chopped
4 eggs, beaten
3 tablespoons skimmed milk
2 x 40g slices dark rye bread
150g young leaf spinach

1 Mist a nonstick frying pan with cooking spray and set over a medium-low heat. Add the spring onions and cook for 2 minutes until softened.

2 Add the eggs and milk, season to taste and cook, stirring often, until the eggs are scrambled and just set.

3 Meanwhile, toast the rye bread and wilt the spinach by putting it into a colander and pouring over a kettle of just-boiled water, then drain well.

4 Top the toast with the eggs and spinach, season to taste and serve.

 SmartPoints value per serving

Potato & bacon tortilla

serves 4   **prep time 30 minutes**   **cook time 35 minutes**

400g potatoes, cut into 5mm
thick slices
50g young leaf spinach
120g bacon medallions
2 teaspoons olive oil
1 small onion, finely chopped
3 eggs, lightly beaten
120g frozen peas
200g reduced-fat cottage cheese
Mixed salad leaves, to serve

1 Put the potatoes in a pan of cold water and bring to the boil. Cook for 5 minutes until tender. Drain and transfer to a large bowl. Add the spinach to the bowl and set aside, covered, for 5 minutes or until the spinach has wilted.

2 Meanwhile, finely chop half the bacon. Put the oil in a nonstick, ovenproof frying pan and set over a medium heat. Add the onion and chopped bacon and cook, stirring, for 6-8 minutes until the onion has softened. Transfer to the bowl with the potato mixture. Add the eggs and mix well.

3 Thinly slice the remaining bacon. Set the frying pan over a medium-high heat, add the sliced bacon and cook, stirring, for 5 minutes or until browned. Transfer to a small bowl.

4 Put the potato mixture into the pan, and spread it out evenly. Cook for 8-10 minutes or until the base is golden and set. Heat the grill to high, then grill the tortilla for 5 minutes or until the top is golden and set.

5 Meanwhile, cook the peas in a pan of boiling water for 2 minutes until tender, then drain, refresh under cold water and drain again. Combine the peas, sliced bacon and cottage cheese in a bowl. Top the tortilla with the cottage cheese mixture, then serve with the salad leaves.

5 SmartPoints value per serving

Eggs Benedict

serves 4 **prep time 5 minutes** **cook time 15 minutes**

8 bacon medallions

6 plum tomatoes, halved

1 teaspoon dried parsley, plus an extra pinch, to serve

4 large eggs

1 teaspoon white wine vinegar

3 tablespoons reduced-fat mayonnaise

1 tablespoon Dijon mustard

Juice of ½ lemon

2 English muffins, halved and toasted

Pinch of paprika, to serve

1 Preheat the oven to 200°C, fan 180°C, gas mark 6 and line a baking sheet with baking paper. Put the bacon and tomato halves on the prepared baking sheet, then season the tomatoes to taste and scatter over the dried parsley. Bake for 10 minutes, then turn the bacon medallions over and cook for another 2-3 minutes until they are golden and the tomatoes are tender.

2 Meanwhile, crack the eggs into a pan of simmering water and poach for about 3 minutes until the whites are just set and the yolks are still soft. Remove from the pan with a slotted spoon and drain on a plate lined with kitchen paper.

3 In a small bowl, whisk the vinegar into the mayonnaise with the mustard and lemon juice, then season to taste. If you need to, add a splash of water to make the hollandaise thin enough to drizzle.

4 Top each muffin half with 2 bacon medallions and a poached egg. Drizzle with the hollandaise, scatter over the extra parsley and the paprika, then serve with the roasted tomatoes.

4 SmartPoints value per serving

Baked French toast

serves 4   **prep time** 20 minutes + soaking   **cook time** 30 minutes

Calorie controlled cooking spray
35g caster sugar
1½ teaspoons ground cinnamon
35g low-fat spread
8 slices WW White Danish Bread
350ml semi-skimmed milk
3 eggs
1 teaspoon vanilla extract
Pinch of salt
200g mixed berries
75g 0% fat natural Greek yogurt

1 Heat the grill to medium. Mist two nonstick baking trays with cooking spray. Combine the sugar and cinnamon in a small bowl. Spread the low-fat spread over each slice of bread, then sprinkle 1 teaspoon of the cinnamon-sugar mixture over each slice. Transfer to the prepared baking trays and grill for 2–3 minutes or until golden and caramelised. Cut each slice in half on the diagonal.

2 Preheat the oven to 190°C, fan 170°C, gas mark 5. Mist a shallow 1-litre baking dish with cooking spray and arrange the toast in two rows, slightly overlapping, in the dish.

3 Whisk together the milk, eggs, vanilla extract and salt in a large jug, then pour the mixture over the toast. Leave to soak for 15 minutes.

4 Sprinkle over the rest of the cinnamon sugar mixture, then bake for 20–25 minutes or until crisp and golden.

5 Serve the toast with the berries and yogurt.

8 SmartPoints value per serving

Boiled eggs with lentil tabbouleh

serves 4   **prep time** 5 minutes   **cook time** 5 minutes

6 eggs

400g tin lentils, rinsed
and drained

Large handful fresh, flat-leaf
parsley, chopped

Handful fresh mint, chopped

2 large tomatoes, chopped

½ red onion, thinly sliced

1 tablespoon olive oil

2 tablespoons lemon juice

60g light feta

2 x 60g wholemeal pitta
breads, halved

1 Bring a pan of water to the boil over a medium-high
heat, then reduce to a simmer. Carefully add the eggs
using a slotted spoon and cook for 3-4 minutes. Drain
the pan then fill again with cold water and set aside for
a few minutes to allow the eggs to cool, then peel.

2 Put the lentils into a medium heatproof bowl. Cover
with boiling water. Set aside for 1 minute, then drain.

3 Put the lentils in a large bowl with the parsley, mint,
tomatoes, red onion, olive oil and lemon juice. Transfer
to a serving platter. Halve the eggs and arrange them
on top of the tabbouleh, then crumble over the feta.

4 Warm the halved pittas in the microwave on high for
20 seconds, then serve with the tabbouleh and eggs.

  SmartPoints value per serving

Cook's tip
Always use a kitchen timer when
soft-boiling eggs, or you run the
risk of over-cooking them.

Prawn pad Thai omelette

serves 1   prep time 20 minutes   cook time 15 minutes

35g dried rice noodles

Calorie controlled cooking spray

75g raw king prawns, peeled and deveined

1 garlic clove, crushed

½ small carrot, cut into matchsticks

1 small red chilli, deseeded and finely sliced

50g bean sprouts

2 spring onions, trimmed and thickly sliced

½ tablespoon sweet soy sauce

Small handful torn fresh Thai basil leaves (or regular basil leaves), plus extra leaves to serve

5g unsalted peanuts, chopped

2 eggs

50ml skimmed milk

1 teaspoon fish sauce

1 Prepare the rice noodles to pack instructions, then refresh under cold running water. Drain and set aside.

2 Mist a large nonstick frying pan with cooking spray and set over a medium-high heat. Cook the prawns and garlic, stirring, for 2 minutes or until the prawns are pink and almost cooked through.

3 Add the carrot, half the chilli, the bean sprouts, spring onions, sweet soy sauce and prepared noodles to the frying pan. Stir-fry for 2-3 minutes, then stir in the torn basil and half the peanuts.

4 Whisk the eggs, milk and fish sauce in a jug until combined. Mist a small nonstick frying pan with cooking spray and set over a medium-high heat. Pour the egg mixture into the pan and cook for 30 seconds or until the base of the omelette is set. Using a spatula, draw the edges of the omelette into the centre to allow any uncooked egg to run underneath. Cook for another 2-3 minutes or until the egg is almost set.

5 Arrange the prawn mixture over half the omelette and fold over to enclose the filling. Serve topped with the remaining chilli and peanuts, and the extra basil leaves.

 **7** SmartPoints value per serving

Butternut squash fritters

serves 4   **prep time** 25 minutes   **cook time** 25 minutes

800g prepared butternut squash, cut into 1cm pieces

80g wholemeal plain flour

1 teaspoon baking powder

20g vegetarian Italian-style hard cheese, grated

1 tablespoon chopped fresh thyme

250g cottage cheese

3 eggs, lightly beaten

2 tablespoons skimmed milk

1 small red onion, thinly sliced

Calorie controlled cooking spray

100g sugar snap peas, thinly sliced

50g pea shoots

80g half-fat créme fraîche

2 tablespoons sweet chilli sauce

1 Cook the butternut squash in a pan of boiling water for 12-15 minutes until tender. Drain. Set aside to cool slightly.

2 Sift the flour and baking powder into a large bowl. Stir in the grated cheese and thyme.

3 Combine the cottage cheese, eggs and milk in a large jug. Pour the mixture into the bowl with the dry ingredients and stir to combine. Stir in the onion and cooked butternut squash.

4 Mist a large nonstick frying pan with cooking spray and set over a medium heat. Make 4 fritters at a time by spooning about 60ml (4 tablespoons) of the batter into the pan for each fritter. Cook for 2-3 minutes on each side or until golden and cooked through. Repeat with remaining batter to make 8 more fritters.

5 Meanwhile, combine the peas and pea shoots in a bowl. For each serving, make a stack of 3 fritters, then top with a quarter of the pea mixture, créme fraîche and sweet chilli sauce, then serve.

 **SmartPoints value per serving**

Egg salad open sandwiches

serves 6   **prep time 20 minutes**   **cook time 15 minutes**

6 large eggs

80g 0% fat natural Greek yogurt

1 spring onion, trimmed and
thinly sliced

2 teaspoons honey mustard

1 teaspoon lemon juice

1 teaspoon finely chopped
fresh tarragon

6 slices WW Thick-Sliced
Wholemeal Bread

Large handful mixed salad leaves

1 avocado, peeled, stone removed
and cut into 12 slices

2 radishes, trimmed and
very thinly sliced

1 Bring a pan of water to the boil over a medium-high heat,
then reduce to a simmer. Carefully add the eggs using a
slotted spoon and cook for 8-10 minutes. Drain, fill the pan
with cold water and set aside for a few minutes to allow the
eggs to cool. Peel and roughly chop.

2 Put the yogurt, spring onion, mustard, lemon juice and
tarragon in a medium bowl and season to taste, then stir
well to combine. Fold in the chopped eggs.

3 Toast the bread, then top each slice of toast with some
salad leaves and 2 avocado slices. Divide the egg mixture
between the toasts, then garnish with the sliced radishes,
season to taste and serve.

 SmartPoints value per serving

Green goodness soup

serves 4   **prep time** 20 minutes   **cook time** 50 minutes

1 tablespoon olive oil

1 leek, thinly sliced

2 garlic cloves, crushed

100g pearl barley

2 litres vegetable stock, made from 4 stock cubes

400g broccoli, cut into small florets

100g kale, chopped

1 courgette, trimmed and spiralised into courgetti

120g frozen peas

4 eggs

20g vegetarian Italian-style hard cheese, grated

1 Heat the oil in a large pan set over a medium heat. Add the leek and cook, stirring, for 3 minutes. Add the garlic and cook for a further minute. Add the barley and stock and bring to a simmer. Cook, partially covered, for 30 minutes, or until the barley is tender. Scoop off any froth from the surface with a spoon.

2 Add the broccoli and kale to the pan and cook for 5 minutes or until just tender. Stir in the courgetti and peas and cook for 2 minutes.

3 Crack the eggs into a pan of simmering water and poach for about 3 minutes until the whites are just set and the yolks are still soft. Remove from the pan with a slotted spoon and drain on a plate lined with kitchen paper.

4 Divide the soup between bowls. Top with the poached eggs and sprinkle over the grated cheese to serve.

 SmartPoints value per serving

Cook's tip

Serve with a 65g crusty bread roll per person for an extra 5 SmartPoints per serving.

Mexican-style crustless quiche

serves 4   **prep time** 10 minutes + cooling   **cook time** 30 minutes

2 eggs
250g quark
25g chorizo, finely diced
60g light feta, crumbled
1 tomato, diced
**3 spring onions, trimmed
and sliced**
1 red pepper, deseeded and diced
¼ teaspoon smoked paprika
½ teaspoon chipotle paste
Juice of ½ lime
50g young leaf spinach, shredded
Calorie controlled cooking spray

1 Preheat the oven to 200°C, fan 180°C, gas mark 6. Lightly whisk the eggs in a large bowl. Beat in the quark until the mixture is smooth.

2 Add all the other ingredients (reserving some of the feta) except the spinach and cooking spray. Season to taste, stir to combine, then fold in the spinach.

3 Mist a 22cm tart tin with cooking spray and pour in the quiche mixture. Top with the reserved feta and bake for 25-30 minutes until golden. Let cool in the tin, then cut into wedges and serve.

 SmartPoints value per serving

Cook's tip
Try serving this with a side salad of mixed leaves, sliced tomatoes and cucumber, for no extra SmartPoints per serving.

Spinach & egg pie

serves 10   **prep time** 30 minutes   **cook time** 1 hour

Calorie controlled cooking spray
1 onion, thinly sliced
3 celery sticks, trimmed and
thinly sliced
1kg young leaf spinach
¼ teaspoon ground allspice
¼ teaspoon ground mace
75g medium-fat soft cheese
20g vegetarian Italian-style hard
cheese, grated
7 eggs
12 sheets filo pastry

1 Mist a large nonstick pan with cooking spray and set over a medium-high heat. Add the onion and celery and cook for 6-8 minutes until the onion is soft and just starting to colour. Add the spinach, then cover and cook for 5 minutes or until the leaves have wilted. Set aside to cool.

2 Preheat the oven to 180°C, fan 160°C, gas mark 4. Line a colander with a clean tea towel and pour in the contents of the pan, then squeeze out as much of the liquid as possible. Transfer to a large bowl and add the spices, soft cheese, grated hard cheese and 1 egg. Set aside.

3 Mist a 21cm springform cake tin with cooking spray. Layer 6 filo sheets inside, misting with cooking spray between each, allowing the edges to hang over the sides of the tin. Tip in the spinach mixture and spread it out evenly.

4 Create 5 wells in the spinach; break an egg into each. Trim the remaining filo sheets so they're slightly larger than the circumference of the pie, then place over the spinach mixture, misting between each sheet and tucking gently down the sides of the spinach. Roll in the overhanging edges. Whisk the remaining egg and brush it over the surface of the pie. Bake for 40 minutes, until cooked and golden brown. Leave to cool for 30 minutes, then serve.

Cook's tip
This pie is just as good served cold. Any leftovers will keep in the fridge for up to 3 days.

5 SmartPoints value per serving

Niçoise salad

serves 2 **prep time** 15 minutes **cook time** 10 minutes

3 large eggs
100g green beans, trimmed
1 yellow pepper, deseeded and cut into strips
100g cherry tomatoes, halved
¼ iceberg lettuce, torn into bite-size pieces
6 pitted black olives in brine, sliced
160g tin tuna in spring water, drained
2 spring onions, trimmed and sliced
½ cucumber, trimmed and diced

FOR THE DRESSING
1 small red chilli, deseeded and finely chopped
4 tablespoons lime juice
1 teaspoon olive oil
1 teaspoon clear honey

1 Bring a pan of water to the boil over a medium-high heat, then reduce to a simmer. Carefully add the eggs using a slotted spoon and cook for 8-10 minutes. Drain, fill the pan with cold water and set aside for a few minutes to allow the eggs to cool. Peel and cut into quarters.

2 While the eggs are cooking, blanch the beans in a separate pan of boiling water for 2 minutes, then drain and transfer to a bowl of cold water until cool. Drain and set aside.

3 Put all the dressing ingredients in a small bowl with 2 tablespoons water, season to taste, then whisk to combine.

4 Put the green beans, pepper, tomatoes, lettuce, olives, tuna, spring onions and cucumber in a serving bowl, then pour over the dressing and toss gently to combine. Divide the salad between 2 plates, top with the boiled egg quarters, then season to taste and serve.

2 SmartPoints value per serving

Salmon & egg slice

serves 8   **prep time** 5 minutes   **cook time** 20 minutes

10 eggs, lightly beaten

60ml skimmed milk

200g ready-prepared stir-fry or coleslaw vegetable mix (see tip)

415g tin red salmon in spring water, drained, skin and bones removed, flaked

Rocket leaves, to serve

1 Preheat the oven to 200°C, fan 180°C, gas mark 6. Line the base and sides of a shallow 30cm x 20cm baking dish with baking paper.

2 Whisk the eggs and milk together in a large bowl until combined. Season to taste and stir through the vegetables. Pour the mixture into the prepared dish. Top with the salmon and bake for 18-20 minutes until set.

3 Using the baking paper, lift the cooked eggs onto a board and cut into 8 slices, then serve with the rocket on the side.

 SmartPoints value per serving

Cook's tip
If you like, you can prepare your own mix of your favourite veg. Just cut them into similar-sized pieces so they cook evenly.

Quiche Lorraine

serves 4   **prep time 15 minutes + cooling**   **cook time 1 hour**

3 WW White Wraps

4 teaspoons sunflower oil

1 large onion, thinly sliced

125g unsmoked bacon medallions, cut into 2cm pieces

4 large eggs

2 tablespoons finely chopped fresh flat-leaf parsley

150ml vegetable stock, made with ¼ stock cube

75g half-fat mature Cheddar, grated

Mixed salad, to serve

1 Preheat the oven to 180°C, fan 160°C, gas mark 4 and heat a baking tray until hot. Brush one side of the wraps with 2 teaspoons of the oil, then microwave each on high for 10 seconds to soften. Press one of the wraps, oil-side-down, into the base of a 20cm cake tin or pie dish. Halve the two remaining wraps, and press around the sides of the tin, making sure they overlap and leave no gaps.

2 Heat the remaining oil in a frying pan set over a medium heat. Add the onion and cook for 6-8 minutes until softened, then stir in the bacon and cook for another 3 minutes.

3 In a bowl, lightly whisk the eggs, then stir in the parsley and stock. Season with freshly ground black pepper.

4 Scatter two-thirds of the cheese over the base of the wrap-lined tin, then spoon over the onion and bacon mixture. Pour over the egg mixture then top with the remaining cheese. Transfer to the hot baking sheet and bake for 40-45 minutes, until the filling is set (see Cook's tip).

5 Cool in the tin or dish for 10 minutes, then cut into wedges and serve with the salad.

Cook's tip
To check the filling is ready, give the tin a little shake – the quiche should have a slight wobble in the middle.

6 SmartPoints value per serving

Salmon kedgeree

serves 2   **prep time** 5 minutes   **cook time** 20 minutes

Calorie controlled cooking spray

1 onion, sliced

2 garlic cloves, crushed

1 teaspoon each of curry power, ground turmeric and ground coriander

100ml fish stock, made with ½ stock cube

40g split red lentils

2 x 130g skinless salmon fillets, cut into thin slices

250g pouch basmati rice

2 eggs

100g asparagus spears, trimmed

1 Mist a large nonstick frying pan with cooking spray and fry the onion, garlic and spices over a medium heat for 2 minutes. Add the stock and lentils and cook for 5 minutes, then add the salmon and cook, stirring, for a further 5 minutes. Stir in the rice and cook for 5 minutes until hot.

2 Meanwhile, bring a pan of water to the boil over a medium-high heat, then reduce to a simmer, carefully add the eggs using a slotted spoon and cook for 5-6 minutes. Drain, fill the pan with cold water and set aside for a few minutes to allow the eggs to cool. Peel and cut into quarters.

3 Cook the asparagus in a pan of boiling water for 2 minutes, then drain.

4 Divide the kedgeree between plates and top with the eggs and asparagus. Season to taste and serve.

 6 SmartPoints value per serving

Asian spiced broth with pork balls

serves 4   **prep time** 20 minutes   **cook time** 30 minutes

400g 5% fat pork mince

3 garlic cloves, finely chopped

4cm piece fresh ginger, peeled and grated

¼ teaspoon ground Szechuan peppercorns

Pinch chilli flakes, plus extra to serve

¼ teaspoon ground cumin

1 teaspoon olive oil

4 eggs

Calorie controlled cooking spray

1 lemongrass stalk, outer layer removed and the rest chopped

2 red chillies, deseeded and finely chopped, plus extra to garnish

1.2 litres chicken stock, made with 1 stock cube

1 star anise

250g mushrooms, sliced

150g Savoy cabbage, shredded

150g broccoli, cut into florets

2 tablespoons soy sauce

1½ teaspoons fish sauce

2 teaspoons hot pepper sauce

Juice of 1 lime

3 spring onions, trimmed and sliced, to serve

1 Mix the pork mince with half the garlic and ginger, all of the peppercorns, chilli flakes and cumin. Form the mixture into 16 balls.

2 Heat the oil in a large, deep nonstick frying pan and cook the balls, in batches, for 5-10 minutes until just golden. Using a slotted spoon, transfer the cooked meatballs to a plate lined with kitchen paper and set aside.

3 Bring a pan of water to the boil over a medium-high heat, then reduce to a simmer, carefully add the eggs using a slotted spoon and cook for 8-10 minutes. Drain, fill the pan with cold water and set aside for a few minutes to allow the eggs to cool, then peel and cut in half.

4 Mist the frying pan with cooking spray and set over a medium heat. Cook the remaining garlic and ginger, the lemongrass and chillies for 2 minutes. Stir in the stock and star anise, bring to the boil, then reduce to a simmer.

5 Add the mushrooms, cabbage and broccoli, then return the meatballs to the pan. Cook for 5 minutes, then stir in the soy, fish and hot pepper sauces and the lime juice. Serve the soup topped with the eggs, spring onions and extra chilli flakes.

 **SmartPoints value per serving**

Speedy spaghetti carbonara

serves 4   **prep time 10 minutes**   **cook time 15 minutes**

300g spaghetti

Calorie controlled cooking spray

4 rashers back bacon, chopped

250g mushrooms, sliced

1 spring onion, trimmed and
finely chopped

1 garlic clove, halved

250g medium-fat soft cheese
with herbs

1 egg

150ml skimmed milk

30g Parmesan cheese, grated

2 tablespoons very finely
chopped fresh flat-leaf parsley,
to serve

1 Cook the pasta to pack instructions, or until al dente.
Drain, reserving 100ml of the cooking water.

2 Meanwhile, set a large nonstick frying pan over a
medium heat and mist with cooking spray. Add the
bacon, mushrooms, spring onion and garlic, and cook for
5 minutes, until softened. Remove and discard the garlic.

3 In a mixing bowl, combine the soft cheese and egg, then
stir in the bacon mixture, the milk, half of the Parmesan
and the parsley. Season to taste. Put the spaghetti in a
pan set over a low heat, add the cheese mixture and heat
for 2-3 minutes, stirring, until the mixture has thickened.
Add a little of the reserved pasta water to form a sauce.

4 Divide the spaghetti between 4 plates and serve topped
with the remaining Parmesan.

 **15** SmartPoints value per serving

Florentine pizza

serves 2   **prep time 10 minutes**   **cook time 25 minutes**

180g self-raising flour

200g 0% fat natural Greek yogurt

80g young leaf spinach

100g passata

2 garlic cloves, crushed

2 tablespoons roughly torn fresh basil

80g light mozzarella, sliced

2 teaspoons dried oregano

2 eggs

Mixed salad leaves, to serve

1 Preheat the oven to 220°C, fan 200°C, gas mark 7 and put a large baking sheet in the oven to heat up. In a medium bowl, combine the flour and yogurt to form a dough. Divide the dough in half, then roll out each piece on a sheet of baking paper to form a 15cm-diameter circle, then transfer the pizza bases (on the baking paper) to the preheated tray. Bake for 10 minutes.

2 Meanwhile, set a large lidded frying pan over a medium heat. Add the spinach, then cover and cook for 2-3 minutes until just wilted. Drain.

3 In a small bowl, combine the passata, garlic, and basil and season to taste. Spoon the sauce over the pizza bases, leaving a border around the edge.

4 Scatter over the mozzarella, wilted spinach, oregano and some freshly ground black pepper, leaving a space in the centre. Carefully crack an egg into the space on each base. Reduce the oven temperature to 200°C, fan 180°C, gas mark 6, then return the pizzas to the oven and cook for 8-10 minutes or until the egg whites are set. Serve the pizzas with the salad.

Cook's tip

Experiment with various veggie toppings – we like butternut squash, red onion and broccoli tossed in za'atar for added spice and flavour.

11 SmartPoints value per serving

Chorizo & tomato pasta

serves 4   **prep time** 10 minutes   **cook time** 15 minutes

240g fusilli pasta
120g frozen peas
100g chorizo, chopped
1 garlic clove, crushed
250g cherry tomatoes, halved
**120g young leaf spinach,
finely shredded**
3 eggs, lightly beaten
**1½ tablespoons
wholegrain mustard**

1 Cook the pasta to pack instructions, adding the peas for the final minute of cooking time, then drain. Set aside.

2 Fry the chorizo in a nonstick frying pan set over a medium-high heat for 3 minutes, or until golden brown.

3 Stir in the garlic and cook for an additional minute, then add the tomatoes, pasta, peas and most of the spinach. Toss together until everything is heated through and the spinach is wilted.

4 Remove the pasta from the heat and immediately stir in the eggs and mustard, allowing the heat from the pasta to cook the eggs and form a creamy sauce. Season to taste and serve topped with the remaining spinach.

Cook's tip
Serve the pasta with a
ZeroPoint mixed leaf salad.

 SmartPoints value per serving

Gammon & egg pie

serves 4   **prep time 20 minutes**   **cook time 55 minutes**

4 eggs

600g potatoes, cut into chunks

1 tablespoon low-fat spread

1 teaspoon wholegrain mustard

300g cooked gammon or ham, cut into chunks

30g half-fat mature Cheddar, grated

Steamed broccoli, to serve

FOR THE SAUCE

1 tablespoon plain flour

2 teaspoons low-fat spread

300ml skimmed milk

50g half-fat mature Cheddar, grated

2 teaspoons wholegrain mustard

2 tablespoons chopped fresh curly-leaf parsley

Cook's tip

Swap the potato mash for celeriac or cauliflower mash for a lighter topping. The SmartPoints will be 8 per serving.

1 Bring a pan of water to the boil over a medium-high heat, then reduce to a simmer, carefully add the eggs using a slotted spoon and cook for 8-10 minutes. Drain, fill the pan with cold water and set aside for a few minutes to allow the eggs to cool, then peel, chop and set aside.

2 Preheat the oven to 190°C, fan 170°C, gas mark 5. Put the potatoes in a pan, cover with cold water and bring to the boil. Cook for 10-15 minutes, or until tender. Drain and mash with the spread and mustard. Season to taste, then set aside.

3 Meanwhile, make the sauce. Put the flour, low-fat spread and milk in a small pan and bring to the boil, whisking constantly. Turn the heat down and cook for another 5 minutes, stirring often, then remove from the heat and stir in the cheese, mustard and parsley. Season to taste.

4 Scatter the gammon or ham over the base of a medium pie dish, then top with the chopped eggs. Pour over the cheese sauce, then spoon over the mash. Scatter over the grated cheese and bake for 30 minutes, until golden and bubbling. Serve with the steamed broccoli on the side.

12 SmartPoints value per serving

Chicken & shiitake egg drop soup

serves 2　**prep time 20 minutes**　**cook time 10 minutes**　

Calorie controlled cooking spray

450g shiitake mushrooms, stems removed and caps sliced

2 teaspoons finely chopped fresh ginger

4 spring onions, trimmed, green and white parts chopped separately

480ml chicken stock, made with 1 stock cube

4 teaspoons reduced-salt soy sauce

1 teaspoon chilli paste, plus an extra 2 teaspoons to serve

230g cooked skinless chicken breast fillets, chopped

½ teaspoon cornflour

2 large eggs, beaten

1　Mist a large pan with cooking spray and set over a medium heat. Add the mushrooms, ginger and the white parts of the spring onions, and cook for 5 minutes, stirring often, until the mushrooms are tender.

2　Add the stock, soy sauce, chilli paste and cooked chicken, then bring the mixture to the boil and cook for 1 minute.

3　In a small bowl, combine the cornflour and 1 teaspoon water. Stir the mixture into the soup, then reduce the heat to a simmer and cook for another 3 minutes.

4　Spoon about 3 tablespoons of the hot soup into a small bowl and stir in the eggs. Slowly pour the egg mixture back into the pan and cook, stirring constantly, for 1 minute. Serve the soup with the green parts of the spring onions scattered over the top and the extra chilli paste on the side for drizzling over.

 SmartPoints value per serving

Cook's tip

To make this soup vegetarian, swap the chicken stock for a vegetable version and the chicken breast fillets for cubed tofu. The SmartPoints will stay the same.

Chicken & egg fried rice

serves 4   prep time 10 minutes   cook time 30 minutes

200g brown rice

4 teaspoons sunflower oil

400g skinless chicken breast fillets, sliced

15g peeled and grated fresh ginger

2 garlic cloves, finely chopped

4 spring onions, trimmed and finely sliced

100g frozen peas, thawed

100g sweetcorn

2 eggs

1 tablespoon soy sauce

Handful fresh coriander, roughly chopped

1 Cook the rice to pack instructions, then drain well and set aside to cool.

2 Put 1 teaspoon of the oil in a wok and set over a medium heat. Add half the chicken and cook for 3-4 minutes or until cooked through. Season to taste and set aside, then repeat with another 1 teaspoon of the oil and the remaining chicken.

3 Reduce the heat to medium-low, add the rest of the oil to the wok and add the ginger, garlic and spring onions. Cook for 1-2 minutes, then add the rice, peas and sweetcorn and heat through. Make a well in the middle and crack in one of the eggs. Gradually work it into the rice mixture, then repeat with the second egg.

4 Add the chicken and soy sauce, mix to combine and cook for 1 minute or until the chicken is warmed through, then serve with the coriander scattered over.

 7 SmartPoints value per serving

Cook's tip

If you have leftover cooked brown rice, this recipe is a great way to use it up. You will need 500g cooked rice.

Spelt pasta with squash & egg

serves 4 **prep time** 10 minutes **cook time** 30 minutes

1 tablespoon olive oil

12 fresh sage leaves

400g butternut squash, cut into 1cm pieces

1 garlic clove, crushed

250g spelt fusilli pasta

400g Tenderstem broccoli, roughly chopped

4 eggs

40g vegetarian Italian-style hard cheese, finely grated, to serve

1 Heat the oil in a lidded pan set over a high heat. Add the sage leaves and cook for 1-2 minutes, or until crisp. Using a slotted spoon, transfer the sage to a plate lined with kitchen paper. Put the squash in the pan and cook, stirring, for 2-3 minutes or until golden. Stir in the garlic, then reduce the heat and cook, covered, for a further 10 minutes, stirring occasionally, until tender.

2 Meanwhile, cook the pasta to pack instructions, or until al dente. Add the broccoli for the final 2 minutes of cooking time, then drain, reserving 2 tablespoons of the cooking water. Return the pasta mixture to the pan, then stir in the cooked squash mixture and the reserved cooking water. Season to taste, then toss gently to combine. Cover and keep warm.

3 Meanwhile, crack the eggs into a pan of simmering water and poach for about 3 minutes until the whites are just set and the yolks are still soft. Remove from the pan with a slotted spoon and drain on a plate lined with kitchen paper.

4 Serve the pasta topped with the poached eggs, grated hard cheese, crispy sage leaves, and seasoning.

Cook's tip

You could use any variety of squash, including cooking pumpkin. The SmartPoints will remain the same.

 **8** SmartPoints value per serving

Egg & lentil curry

serves 4   **prep time 20 minutes**   **cook time 25 minutes**

4 eggs
1 tablespoon olive oil
1 onion, finely chopped
2 garlic cloves, crushed
4 cardamom pods, crushed
2 teaspoons ground coriander
1 teaspoon ground turmeric
1 teaspoon garam masala
¼ teaspoon chilli powder
400g tin chopped tomatoes
125ml vegetable stock, made with 1 stock cube
400g tin green lentils, drained and rinsed
2 courgettes, trimmed and chopped
60g young leaf spinach
4 mini naan breads

1   Bring a pan of water to the boil over a medium-high heat, then reduce to a simmer, carefully add the eggs using a slotted spoon and cook for 8-10 minutes. Drain, fill the pan with cold water and set aside for a few minutes to allow the eggs to cool, then peel and cut into quarters.

2   Meanwhile, heat the oil in a large pan over a medium heat. Add the onion and cook, stirring occasionally, for 6-8 minutes or until soft. Add the garlic and all of the spices and cook, stirring, for another 30 seconds.

3   Stir in the tomatoes, stock, lentils and courgettes. Bring to the boil, then reduce the heat and simmer for 5 minutes, until the courgettes are tender. Stir in the spinach.

4   Divide the lentil curry between 4 bowls and top with the eggs. Serve with the mini naan breads on the side.

 SmartPoints value per serving

Cook's tip
For extra flavour, combine 200g fat-free natural yogurt with 2 tablespoons chopped fresh mint and serve on the side with the naan breads. The SmartPoints will be the same.

Turkey Scotch eggs

makes 8   **prep time 25 minutes + chilling**   **cook time 25 minutes**

9 eggs
1 small onion, finely chopped
1 garlic clove, crushed
500g turkey breast mince
**Handful fresh thyme,
rosemary and parsley
leaves, finely chopped**
**4 tablespoons plain flour, plus
extra for dusting**
50g panko breadcrumbs
1 tablespoon rapeseed oil

1. Bring a pan of water to the boil over a medium-high heat, then reduce to a simmer. Carefully add 8 of the eggs using a slotted spoon and cook for 6-8 minutes. Drain, fill the pan with cold water and set aside for a few minutes to allow the eggs to cool, then peel and pat dry with kitchen paper.

2. Meanwhile, mix together the onion, garlic, turkey mince and herbs.

3. Divide the meat mixture into 8. Dust the work surface with flour, roll each portion of mince into a ball, then flatten into a circle large enough to encase an egg. Put an egg in the centre and use your hands to mould the mince around it so it's completely covered.

4. In a shallow bowl, beat the remaining egg. Put the flour on a plate and the breadcrumbs on a separate plate. Roll each egg in the flour, then the beaten egg and finally the breadcrumbs. Put on a baking tray and chill for 30 minutes.

5. Preheat the oven to 200°C, fan 180°C, gas mark 6. Heat the oil in a frying pan and fry the eggs, in batches, for 1-2 minutes, until starting to turn golden. Transfer to a baking tray and bake for 10-12 minutes until golden.

Cook's tip
Serve with English mustard for an extra 1 SmartPoint per tablespoon.

 SmartPoints value per serving

Hash brown, sausage & egg cups

makes 12   **prep time** 15 minutes + soaking & resting   **cook time** 35 minutes

850g King Edward potatoes, peeled and grated
Calorie controlled cooking spray
1 small onion, finely diced
1 teaspoon fennel seeds
1 garlic clove, crushed
250g 5% fat pork mince
5 sage leaves, finely shredded
10 eggs, whisked until foamy
Fresh chives, snipped, to garnish

1 Soak the grated potato in water for 1 hour, then drain, rinse and drain again. Squeeze out any excess liquid with your hands, then pat dry with kitchen paper.

2 Mist a 12-hole nonstick muffin tin with cooking spray. Line each hole with baking paper, then mist again.

3 Preheat the oven to 200°C, fan 180°C, gas mark 6. Put the potato in a microwave-safe bowl and cook on high for 2 minutes, stirring halfway. Season then press into the base and sides of the prepared muffin tin to line. Bake for 15 minutes until golden.

4 Meanwhile, mist a nonstick frying pan with cooking spray and cook the onion and fennel seeds over a medium-low heat for 5 minutes. Add the garlic and cook for another minute, then add the pork and cook for 6-8 minutes. Stir in the sage and season.

5 Spoon the mince mixture into the potato cases, then pour over the eggs. Season to taste and bake for 15 minutes until puffed up. Rest for 10 minutes, then remove from the tin and serve garnished with the chives.

Cook's tip
The hash brown cups will keep for 2-3 days in a sealed container in the fridge.

2 SmartPoints value per serving

3-ingredient pancakes

serves 1   **prep time 10 minutes**   **cook time 5 minutes**

2 small ripe bananas

1 egg

2 tablespoons wholemeal self-raising flour

Calorie controlled cooking spray

2 teaspoons low-fat spread

Pinch of cinnamon, plus extra to serve

1 Put one of the bananas in a small bowl and mash until smooth. Whisk in the egg, then stir in the flour until you have a smooth batter. Set aside for 5 minutes.

2 Mist a medium nonstick frying pan with cooking spray and set over a medium heat. Spoon 2 tablespoons of batter into the pan and spread out with the back of a spoon until 1cm thick. Repeat with the remaining batter to make 2 more pancakes.

3 Cook for 1–2 minutes on each side, or until the pancakes are golden and cooked through.

Cook's tip

Instead of the spread topping, add a handful of blueberries to the pancakes before flipping, then serve with more berries and a teaspoon of honey for the same SmartPoints.

4 Slice the remaining banana. In a small bowl, combine the low-fat spread with a pinch of cinnamon. Serve the pancakes topped with the sliced banana, the cinnamon spread and an extra sprinkling of cinnamon.

 SmartPoints value per serving

Custard tarts

makes 8   prep time 15 minutes + chilling   cook time 40 minutes

375g light shortcrust
pastry sheet (220g used)
2 eggs
45g caster sugar
300ml skimmed milk
¼ teaspoon grated nutmeg

1   Preheat the oven to 200°C, fan 180°C, gas mark 6. Roll the pastry out to the thickness of a pound coin, then use a 10cm cookie cutter to cut out 8 rounds. Discard the pastry trimmings. Use the pastry rounds to line 8 holes of a muffin tin, then chill the pastry for 30 minutes.

2   Line each pastry case with a small piece of baking paper (it helps if you crumple the paper up first), then fill with baking beans. Bake for 10 minutes, then remove the paper and beans and bake for a further 5 minutes, or until the pastry is a light golden colour.

3   Reduce the oven temperature to 180°C, fan 160°C, gas mark 4. Beat the eggs and caster sugar together in a large bowl. Gently heat the milk over a low heat and pour it over the egg mixture. Beat well, then strain through a fine mesh sieve into a jug. Stir in half the nutmeg. Carefully pour the custard into the pastry cases, sprinkle over the remaining nutmeg and bake for 25 minutes or until just set. Allow to cool completely, then remove from the tin and serve.

Cook's tip
For a flavour variation, try adding the grated zest of an orange or lemon to the custard mixture.

5   SmartPoints value per tart

Dark chocolate-orange mousse

makes 8   prep time 30 minutes + chilling

**3 large egg whites
(you'll need 120g)**

30g icing sugar

115g dark chocolate chips

**175g 0% fat natural
Greek yogurt**

½ teaspoon grated orange zest

**25g pistachio kernels,
roughly chopped**

1 Using a hand-held electric whisk, beat the egg whites
and sugar together on a low speed until the sugar has
dissolved. Increase the speed and beat, scraping down
the sides, until stiff peaks form – this should take about
10 minutes.

2 Put the chocolate chips in a medium heatproof bowl and
pour over 80ml boiling water from the kettle. Let stand
for 30 seconds, then stir until the chocolate is melted and
the mixture is smooth. Set the bowl of melted chocolate
over a large bowl filled with ice water and whisk for 2-3
minutes, or until thickened slightly.

3 Remove the bowl of whipped chocolate from the bowl
of ice water, then fold in the Greek yogurt, orange zest
and a large spoonful of the beaten egg whites. Fold in the
remaining egg whites until just combined.

4 Divide the mousse between 8 small dessert glasses, then
chill in the fridge for 2 hours, or until set. Scatter over the
chopped pistachios just before serving.

5 SmartPoints value per serving

Zingy lemon meringue tart

serves 12   prep time 25 minutes + cooling   cook time 40 minutes

200g ginger nut biscuits
75g apple sauce
1 lemon (peel left on)
30ml freshly squeezed lemon juice
225g caster sugar
1 tablespoon cornflour
3 egg yolks
2 egg whites

1 Preheat the oven to 200°C, fan 180°C, gas mark 6. In a food processor, blitz the ginger nuts to crumbs. Add the apple sauce and pulse until the mixture comes together. Tip into a 36cm x 12cm loose-bottomed tart tin and press into the corners and up the sides. Bake for 10 minutes. Remove and reduce the temperature to 180°C, fan 160°C, gas mark 4.

2 Wash the lemon, then chop into chunks, discarding any seeds. Wipe the food processor clean, then add the lemon. Process until it has completely broken down, then add the lemon juice, 125g of the sugar, the cornflour and egg yolks. Process until you have a thick, pale yellow mixture.

3 Set a small heatproof bowl over a pan of simmering water. Pour the lemon mixture into the bowl and stir continuously for 5 minutes, until heated through. Pour into the baked biscuit case, then transfer to a baking tray.

4 Whisk the egg whites until soft peaks form. Gradually add the remaining sugar, whisking constantly, until you have a thick, glossy meringue. Spoon into a piping bag fitted with a star-shaped nozzle and pipe 12 rows on top of the tart.

5 Bake for 25 minutes until the meringue is golden. Remove from the oven and let cool for 3 hours, then slice and serve.

8 **SmartPoints value per serving**

Index

SmartPoints index

Seven℃³

Produced by Seven Publishing on behalf of WW International, Inc. Published April 2019. All rights reserved. No part of this publication may be reproduced, stored in retrieval system or transmitted in any form by any means, electronic, mechanical photocopying, recording or otherwise, without the prior written permission of Seven Publishing. First published in Great Britain by Seven Publishing Ltd.

Seven Publishing Ltd,
3-7 Herbal Hill, London EC1R 5EJ
www.seven.co.uk

A CIP catalogue record for this book is available from the British Library.

ISBN: 978-1-9996673-4-4

WW PUBLISHING TEAM
Samantha Rees, Harriet Joy,
Ruby Bamford, Nicola Kirk

FOR SEVEN PUBLISHING LTD
FOOD
Food editor: Nadine Brown

EDITORIAL
Editor-in-Chief: Helen Renshaw
Editor: Ward Hellewell
Sub-editor: Sarah Nittinger

DESIGN & PHOTOGRAPHY
Art director: Liz Baird
Photographers: Steve Baxter,
Florian Bonanni, Steve Brown,
Ant Duncan, Dan Jones,
Jonathan Kennedy, Kris Kirkham,
Vanessa Levis, Andy Lewis,
Alex Luck, David Malosh,
Lauren Mclean, Cath Muscat,
Ria Osborne, Hubertus Schüler,
Kate Sears, Rob Shaw,
John Paul Urizar

ACCOUNT MANAGEMENT
Account manager: Gina Cavaciuti
Group publishing director:
Kirsten Price

PRODUCTION
Senior production manager:
Liz Knipe
Colour reproduction by F1 Colour
Printed in the UK by CPI Colour